THE BIG BOOK OF
CATS

THE BIG BOOK OF

CATS

TEXT BY GLADYS EMERSON COOK
AND FELIX SUTTON
ILLUSTRATIONS BY
GLADYS EMERSON COOK

GROSSET & DUNLAP · Publishers · New York

Copyright 1954 by Gladys Emerson Cook. Lithographed in the United States of America.
ISBN: 0-448-00339-2 (Trade Edition)
ISBN: 0-448-03726-2 (Library Edition)
1975 PRINTING

THE TABBY CAT

Many people use the word "Tabby" to describe any mother cat with kittens. Actually, the Tabby is a distinct breed and is a gentle and intelligent household pet. The broad stripes and blotches of his or her markings resemble a kind of watered silk, called *atabi,* that has been woven for many centuries in Bagdad, Iraq. This is how the Tabby is said to have gotten his name. Some people, however, believe that the Tabby originally came from an island off the coast of Egypt, called Tabbe.

The true Tabby has broad black stripes running down his back, swirls or blotches on his sides, and a "butterfly" on each shoulder. He has rings around his tail, "bracelets" around his legs, and "necklaces" around his neck. His forehead is decorated with the letter M.

When a Tabby has stripes running down his sides instead of swirls and blotches, he is called a Tiger Tabby, or a Tiger Cat. The Tiger Cat also has "bracelets" and "necklaces." If the stripes are broken, he is known as a Broken Tiger or Mackerel Tabby.

THE SIAMESE CAT

As their name indicates, Siamese cats came originally from Siam, or Thailand, as it is now called. They are sometimes known as Royal cats, Sacred cats or Temple cats.

The first Siamese cats were introduced into England in 1884 and into America about ten years later. They have become so popular that they are now more numerous in other countries than in their native land.

Siamese kittens are pure white at birth. As they grow older, they develop the peculiar markings, or "points," that distinguish the Siamese cat.

There are two types of Siamese: the "seal point" and the "blue point." The "seal point" has a light, fawn-colored body and dark brown ears, legs, paws, tail and face. The body of the "blue point" is a light bluish gray, and his "points" are also bluish gray, but much darker than his body.

The long, narrow head and slanting deep blue eyes of the Siamese cat give him an oriental look.

Because Siamese cats have been kept as household pets for thousands of years, they are extremely affectionate and are entirely dependent upon human care.

THE PERSIAN CAT

Persian cats are the "beauties" of the cat world. They are always decorative, and always appear to be well aware of their beauty. A Persian will enter a room gracefully, with his gorgeous plume tail held high, as though demanding the admiration of everyone present.

With the people who own him, a Persian is usually very affectionate. But with strangers, he is often inclined to be snobbish and unfriendly. In spite of their elegant appearance, most Persians are excellent mousers and sometimes they make good "watchcats."

THE BURMESE CAT

The Burmese cat is one of the oldest of all breeds. In Burma, in ancient times, this breed was considered sacred and was owned only by the priests and by very wealthy people. Each cat is said to have had his own personal servant to take care of him.

Even today, these cats are never sold in Burma. The only ones that leave the country are given as gifts to visiting friends.

The Burmese cat looks very much like the Siamese, except that he is smaller. His coat is an extremely smooth and velvety brown and his eyes are golden.

Burmese cats are lovable, gentle and make fine pets. They are easily housebroken and are not usually destructive.

THE ABYSSINIAN CAT

The Abyssinian is also one of the oldest breeds of cat. He dates back to the days of ancient Egypt. There he was worshiped as a god. In fact, the Abyssinian cat of today, with his long, pointed ears and long, slender legs, looks very much like the Egyptian cats that were pictured in the carvings on ancient Egyptian tombs.

Historians say that the word "puss" comes from Pasht, the name of an Egyptian goddess who had the body of a human being and the head of a cat.

The Abyssinian cat is slender and graceful, with a pointed head and a long, tapering tail. His coat is gray-brown or red-brown and at the end of each hair there is a spot of dark brown. This causes the strange mottled effect that is characteristic of the breed.

Abyssinian cats have sweet dispositions and gentle manners. This makes them ideal pets for children. The breed is a very rare one and we do not often see these cats in the United States.

THE TORTOISE-SHELL CAT

Tortoise-shell cats are so named because of their coloring, which has the red, black and cream patterns of the shell of a tortoise. In some rural parts of this country, they are called calico cats.

Almost all cats born with Tortoise-shell markings are females. Males are so rare that thousands of dollars have been offered for one. As far as it is known, there is only one male Tortoise-shell cat in the United States today.

THE MALTESE CAT

Maltese cats come from Malta, an island in the Mediterranean Sea. During the days of the **Crusades**, Malta was a stronghold for Christian knights who went from Europe to fight in the Middle East. It is thought that these knights brought the first Maltese cats back with them from the Asiatic countries and kept them on the island as pets. The Maltese cat is a light blue-gray in color. His nose is usually blue and his eyes are orange or copper. Most short-haired blue cats are called Maltese.

THE RUSSIAN BLUE

These handsome blue cats originally came from the northern part of Russia and that is how they got their name. They are usually a deeper, more lavender blue than the Maltese, and their legs and tails are longer. Although short-haired, the Russian Blue's coat is fine and silky and shines like silver when the light strikes it. Russian Blues are very rare in the United States.

THE MAINE COON CAT

No one can be sure just where the Coon cat came from. But the story is told that during the French Revolution, Queen Marie Antoinette planned to escape to the United States. She had her agents buy a house in a little town in Maine. Among the possessions that she planned to take with her were six beautiful Persian cats.

Marie Antoinette, of course, never left France, for she was captured by the Revolutionaries and killed. When the ship that carried her belongings arrived in Maine, the Captain did not know what to do with the cats. So he turned them loose. The cats mated with the short-haired Tabbies in Maine. The result was the lovely, long-haired cat with the tiger markings called the Maine Coon cat.

New England farmers, seeing them running in the fields, thought they were raccoons. And that is how they got their name.

THE MANX CAT

The Manx cat is one of the few four-legged animals in the world that has no trace of a tail. Instead, he has a slight depression in the back of his spine where the tail should begin.

The Manx comes from the Isle of Man, a small island off the coast of England in the Irish Sea. Many stories are told about his origin. The most accepted story is that when the Spanish Armada was wrecked off the English coast in 1588, some tailless cats that probably had come from the Far East were able to swim ashore. All Manx cats are said to have descended from these shipwrecked cats.

The coloring of the Manx is usually like that of the Tabby. But there are many that have solid coloring. The Manx can run very fast and is a famous ratter and mouser.

INTERESTING THINGS EVERYONE

The word for "cat" is nearly the same in almost every language. In French, it is *chat;* in German, *kat;* in Spanish, *gata;* in ancient Egyptian, *kut.* You could go almost anywhere in the world and be understood if you spoke the word "cat." The cat has one of the most delicate senses of touch of all the animals in the world. He feels not only with his whiskers, but with every hair on his body. Next time you pet your cat, notice that his first reaction is to recoil from your touch. Then when the first shock is over, he will rub against you and ask you to keep on stroking his fur.

A cat expresses his feelings with his purr, his paws, his fur, his eyes, his ears and his tail. If he is curious about something, he points his ears in that direction, looks at the object intently, touches it gingerly with his front paws and waves his tail slowly back and forth. If a cat is angry, he spits and growls and lashes his tail like a lion. When he is frightened, the fur on his tail puffs up and the hair along his back stands on end. If a cat is happy, he purrs with contentment. If a cat wants to get your attention, he meows. Cats are said to express more kinds of emotion than any other animal — jealousy, selfishness and particularly, curiosity. A cat loves deeply and suffers deeply.

If you own a long-haired cat, it is good to brush his coat every day. Even short-haired cats should be brushed from time to time. A cat swallows most of the hairs that he licks from his coat when washing himself. These can form a ball of hair in the cat's stomach that can make him very ill.

HOULD KNOW ABOUT CATS

A cat has a natural instinct for landing on his feet when he falls, even if dropped from a height of only a foot.

Cats walk on their toes and the soles of their feet. Their heels are well developed, but they never touch the ground. Five toes are usual on the forefeet and four on the hind feet. Some cats may have as many as seven toes in front and six toes in back, and these cats are very highly prized.

Most cats are natural retrievers. With a little patience, they can be taught to fetch a thrown ball as easily as a dog.

Cats are very self-conscious. A cat always likes to be seen at his best and therefore is easily embarrassed. If a cat does an ungraceful thing — such as bumping into an unexpected object, or making a clumsy landing when he jumps or falls — he will at once hide his embarrassment by washing his face. Also, if a cat is undecided about what to do, he will wash. His motto seems to be: *"When in doubt, wash!"*

Some cats live to a very old age. The oldest cat on record lived to be thirty-one. This is equal, in the human life span, to one hundred and three.

Sometimes a cat will seem very anxious to go out of the house. But when you open the door, he will stand on the doorsill for several minutes as though trying to decide what to do. This does not mean that the cat has changed his mind and doesn't want to go out after all. It is simply a throw-back to early times when cats were wild and lived in caves. They had to make sure there were no enemies about before they left the safety of the den.

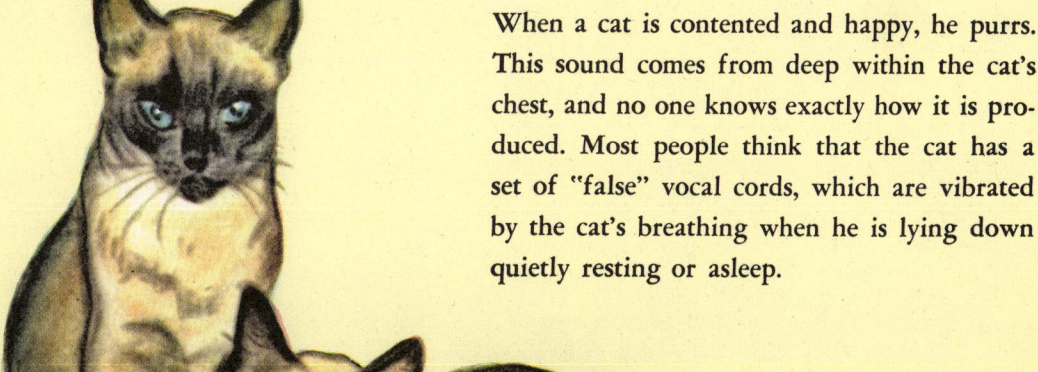

When a cat is contented and happy, he purrs. This sound comes from deep within the cat's chest, and no one knows exactly how it is produced. Most people think that the cat has a set of "false" vocal cords, which are vibrated by the cat's breathing when he is lying down quietly resting or asleep.

THE ANGORA CAT

Today it is very hard to find a true Angora cat. These beautiful animals came originally from the province of Angora, now called Ankara, high in the mountains of Turkey. This is a region famous for long-haired goats and dogs, as well as long-haired cats.

In recent years, Angoras have been crossbred with Persians, and now there is no distinction between the two breeds. Both are shown in cat shows as "long-haired" cats.

The true Angora's long, silken fur is finer and softer than that of the Persian. His body is longer and slimmer, his legs are considerably longer, and his head is thinner and more pointed.

SOLID-COLOR CATS

Some cats of both long-haired and short-haired breeds have coats of a solid color. These are usually black, white or red. In olden times, solid-color cats were thought to have magical powers. White cats were supposed to bring good luck, and black cats bad luck. Even today, some people will cross the street to keep a black cat from walking in front of them. But this is just a silly superstition. Many a child has a lovable black kitten for a pet and plays with it every day without having any bad luck because of it. White cats usually have blue or green eyes. Black cats generally have orange eyes, and the red cat's eyes are ordinarily amber.

SHORT-HAIRED CATS

Of all the many kinds of cats in the world, the most common are the short-hairs. This is the breed that is usually referred to as "alley cats," but their ancestry goes back much farther than their fancier long-haired cousins, the Persians and Angoras. Short-haired cats are often stronger, quicker and more vigorous than the long-haired breeds. Being more closely related to the wild cats of the jungle, they are usually better mousers and hunters.

TRAINING YOUR CAT

As a rule, a cat requires much less training than a dog. Kittens are usually taught to behave by their mothers. Rarely do they need to be housebroken. Cats are naturally clean animals and they seem to behave themselves by instinct. However, there are a few things you should know in order to help your kitten learn good manners. When holding a cat, always place one hand under his body. Never lift a cat by his front legs. And *never* lift him by the skin on the back of his neck. The mother cat carries her kittens this way, but *she* knows how to do it without hurting them. *You* don't!

The first thing you should provide for your kitten is a nice soft bed. This can be a box, a basket or a cardboard carton. Place a folded towel or blanket in the bottom of the box and change it whenever it begins to get dirty. All cats dislike dirt of any kind. If you provide a pleasant bed for your kitten, he will not be tempted to spend his nights on the furniture.

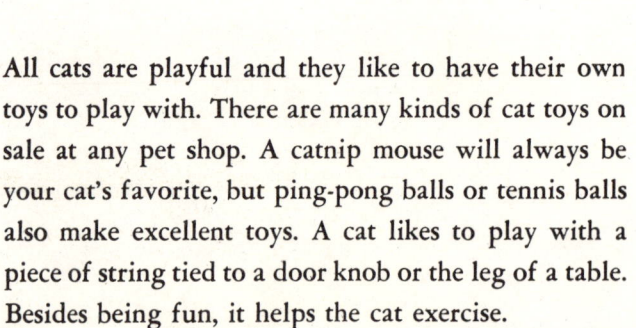

All cats are playful and they like to have their own toys to play with. There are many kinds of cat toys on sale at any pet shop. A catnip mouse will always be your cat's favorite, but ping-pong balls or tennis balls also make excellent toys. A cat likes to play with a piece of string tied to a door knob or the leg of a table. Besides being fun, it helps the cat exercise.

The first day you get your kitten, you should provide a metal sanitary pan for him. This pan should be about two inches deep and filled with torn paper or sand.

Be sure that you clean and refill the pan every day. If you leave it dirty, your cat may refuse to use it. Put your kitten into the pan and make him stay there until he uses the pan. Once your kitten has done this, it will become a habit, and he will never give you any trouble.

Every cat should have a scratching post. Cats keep their claws healthy by scratching at hard surfaces. When you introduce your cat to his scratching post for the first time, help him put his claws on the post and encourage him to scratch. As soon as your cat knows that the post is his very own, the furniture is saved. If a mother cat is about to have kittens, provide a large box for her to keep them in, and line it with an old soft wool or cotton blanket. Be sure to put the box in an out-of-the-way place that is fairly warm and dark. Mother cats like privacy. Place her in the box, so that she understands that this is where she is to have her kittens and take care of them. Put a pan of water and another of milk near the box. Cats rarely have any trouble giving birth to their babies. So it is best to leave a mother cat alone and let her take care of herself until the kittens are born.

If you have more than one cat in the house, each should be given his own food bowl. This assures every one of your pets of getting a full share of food.

OCELOT

TIGER

JAGUAR

THE GREAT WILD CATS of the jungle are first cousins of the gentle Tabby that sleeps peacefully on your hearth at home.

The Big Cats are considered to be extremely dangerous wild animals, and are so strong that a big lion or tiger can carry a full-grown ox in its mouth. The tiger is found in Asia, and the lion and leopard are found in Asia and Africa. The cheetah lives in India, and is sometimes trained for hunting. The ocelot and jaguar are natives of Central and South America.